Oblivion

First paperback edition March 2022

Book design by Reilly Ballantyne
Illustrations by Siham Karamali
Edited by Shelly Zevlever

ISBN: 978-1-7779848-0-9 (paperback)
ISBN: 978-1-7779848-1-6 (eBook)

Plume Press is an imprint of Plume,
a product of The Soap Box Press

Plume
Toronto, Ontario
www.plumepress.com

Oblivion

by Lamia Firasta

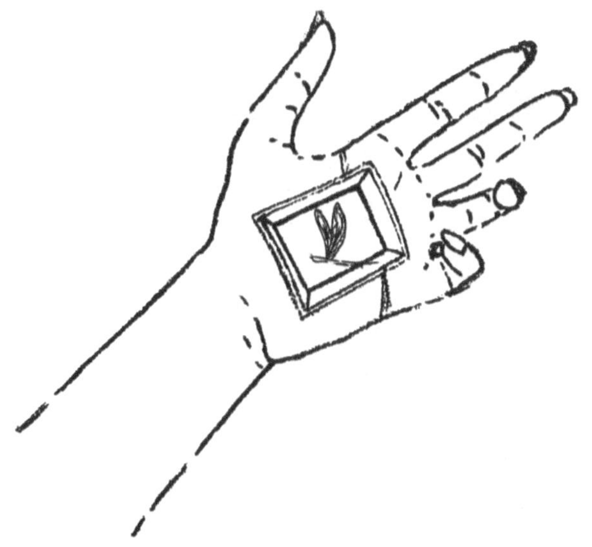

To all the boys and girls who didn't stay
Don't worry
You live in these pages

Stories are not just something we listen to with tea and forget.
My story is not just a story you listen to with tea and forget.
Your story is not just a story you listen to with tea and forget.

We are more than just our stories.

We are beings with magic in our minds and wands at our fingertips. We are entities full of possibilities. Our life is not just what "he said" or "she said". Life is full of learning and unlearning who you are. Sometimes we become art that will never be appreciated in its own generation. Life is full of ups and downs and you have the choice to change or watch from afar. Pen and paper became my best friend ever since I could learn to write and in its own way writing became a healing process for me. Even if one percent of my story resonates with yours, I have to share it with you because you know you're not the only one who feels this way. If I can connect to you through my words, I am fulfilling my purpose in this world.

GROUP EFFORT

Oh child
I know
You're hurt
You think all these girls and boys
Aren't hurting?
All of life is hurt
Shh but wait.
Hurt is not a gift
We don't pass hurt to others in a
Cycle
Your hurting won't end by hurting others
Oh child
We're all hurt
But don't pass around pain
Share your pain and
Heal together

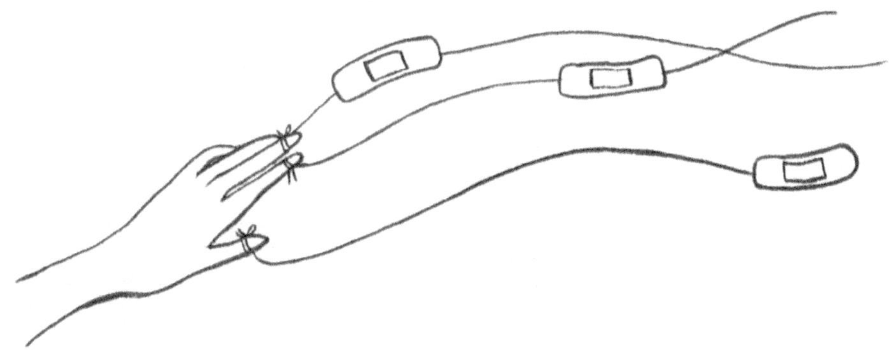

UNCONSCIOUS

We sit so close to oblivion
Where we do things without thinking
We speak without listening
We act without understanding
Never questioning the system
Until we realize there is blood
That is no longer red
Now black because our heart
No longer wants to beat
Our breath has become so shallow
That it lives in our bones
Flows in our blood
We don't recognize ourselves
Anymore
We are *oblivion*

SONDER

I see people on the train
Some reading
Some falling
Into a book
Into the window
Into their phone
Each cabin is full of stories
And at every station
The stories change
Each window holds so many looks we couldn't give to others
Each seat carries the weight of an infinite amount of people
We sit so close to so many heroes
That we don't know
It's where oblivion stops but never ends

PORCELAIN CIRCUMSTANCE

I grew up in a white neighborhood
Thinking that was a good thing
Until you started making fun
Of my clothes, my food
You were repulsed by our smell
I had to learn the ways of your fair skin

Just to be acknowledged
My South Asian friend would eat lunch
Holding up the container lid as a shield
Slowly she started bringing pasta for lunch
Now, years later
The same porcelain dolls
Will drink Chai tea lattes and eat butter chicken
And make DIY turmeric lattes
I'll find you buying naan at the supermarket
You now find *curry* boys pretty
Then use spray tan to look like me
Now that my culture is popular how could you—
How dare you—
Steal from the culture you once shamed me for?

- *Porcelain circumstance was originally published in The Hyphenated*
  Generation published by The Soap Box Press in 2021

AROUND THE BLOCK

It's Friday and I'm passing the station
But right above the station steps
Lies a young man standing
Most likely in his twenties
Trying to run away from life
Contemplating the feeble jump.
Only a few people notice
One lady says "*you don't want to do this*"
In an attempt to comfort him and I think
There's so much to live for than just this one jump
100 meters down
But then right around the corner
There are some people in blue vests striking up a conversation
About how some girls don't have access to education
But my money can help
And my blood *boils*
It *curdles*
I think
There is a young man going to commit suicide and
Only five people noticed
Yet 20 people in blue vests picket for education in third world countries
I guess I should donate all my money to this cause so that will fix one
Problem
But what about that boy who's going to jump right around the corner
Just ignore him?
We're too focused on changing the world
So he is irrelevant
Making this big change in faraway places
Helping people we don't even know
But what about our own?
No one realizes
What if change is right around the block
But maybe just maybe a revolution is just waiting to happen
If we stop that boy from falling

~Queens Park Station

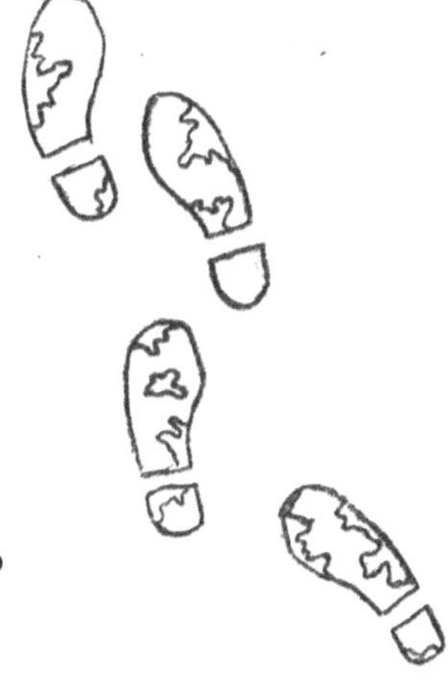

INFLUENCERS

Wanting to die
Is not a video title
Or a popular trend.
Pulling the mental health card
Is not a marketing tool
Or damage control.
Depression
Is real
And shamed.

It's when you tell your parents you're depressed and
They gaslight you.
Anxiety
Isn't just in your head.
It's raw,
It's when you tell your friends you're anxious
And you hear get over it.
Self-Harm is not a personality trait.
It's cutting yourself and wearing long sleeves
Years later because you're ashamed of the scars.
Anorexia
Is not aesthetic.
It's looking in the mirror and not recognizing yourself anymore
Eating disorders
Are not an excuse.
It's stress eating because no one is there for you except food.
It's weighing yourself every morning and taking laxatives so you can lose
Weight.
Mental health is in you and me
It's in everyone
But please oh please
I beg you
Please don't make it entertainment

JANUARY 29

Let's talk
You know what
Let's actually talk
About how men aren't allowed to express their feelings
Because if they do
He's a boy
Not manly enough
As if he wasn't born into this world crying
As if depression is just handpicked for
Women
Let's talk about how women aren't allowed
To get angry
Because if they do
She's a girl
Throwing a temper tantrum
Let's actually talk
About how depression is a silent disease
And anxiety its lover
Both go hand in hand
So how about tomorrow
Just maybe let's talk for more than just one
Day
Let's talk
every day

~ Response to Bell Let's Talk Day

CONFINED

How can I write with freedom
When everyone knows I'm depressed
And ask me at every corner what happened
How can I write openly
When people know I'm heartbroken
And offer their shoulder to cry on
How can I write truly
When everyone knows I'm angry
And tells me to calm down
How can I write freely
When everyone has something to say
How can I be true to myself
If I have to censor my poetry
And justify my inspiration
How can I write
When I'm told to keep the hurt in
My belly and not in my words
This isn't freedom
If I'm kidnapped
By my own words

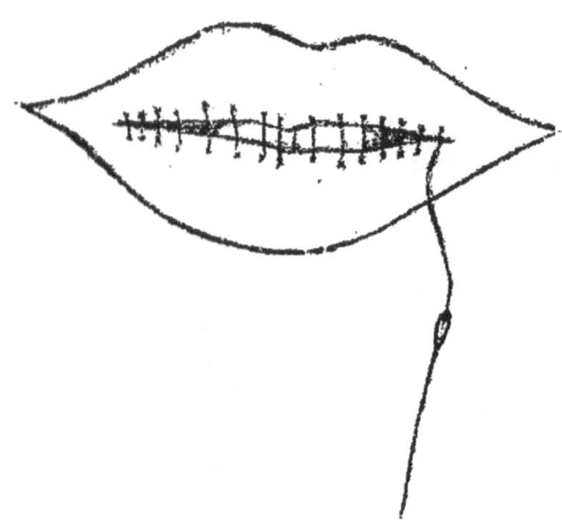

SELF-HATE

Why did it take a boy
For me to learn that my body is beautiful
That I am worthy of love
Why didn't I know that
Why did I need a boy to teach me
Why?
How did I not know that?
How was I so oblivious
20 years went by without me knowing my worth
How is God okay with that

-Perplexed

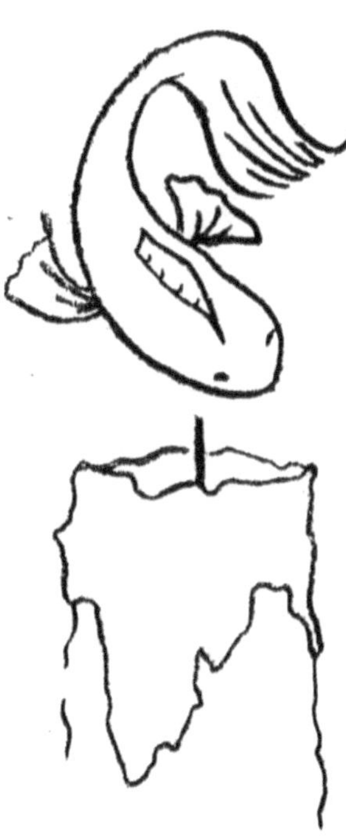

UNANSWERED

Why am I still so good to those
Who wrong me
Like I can't draw the line
I can't be rude to those who are
I don't have that kind of bone
But I get so mad
Just because I am soft
Doesn't mean I don't
Get
Angry
It rages me
I want to set fire to my steps
I want to cry
No tears
No sorrow
but
Flames
I want you to see flames
So they burn your eyes
And you never strike a match
With
Me
Again
But all I do is sigh
Because my rage isn't worth your
Indifference

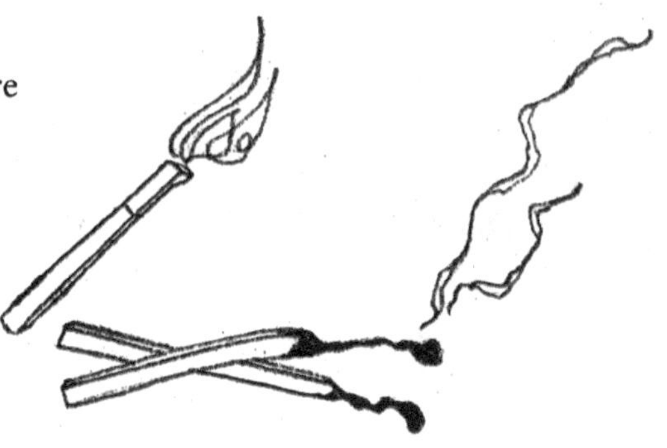

STORY TIME

Listen come around
Sit down
Give me your attention
I'll tell you the story
That most women don't
Ever mouth
That we never hear
One that's buried underneath the stones
Underneath the grass
One where a newly married wife
Is bullied
By her mother
In law
Tortured
Broken
By a mother
That isn't their own
It's fantasized on the TV screen
But torturous in reality
And yet this cycle repeats
Women are against each other
Are jealous of each other
Manipulate others
Play games
Spill white lies
This story needs to be told
Spoken far and wide
So no woman ever bullies another again

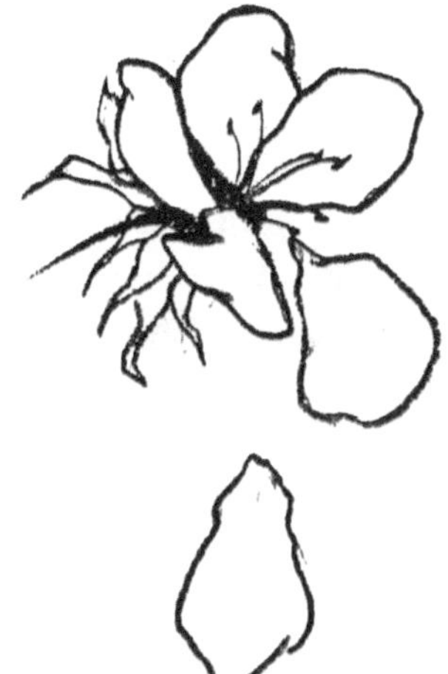

~Words my mother wished to say but came out in her daughter

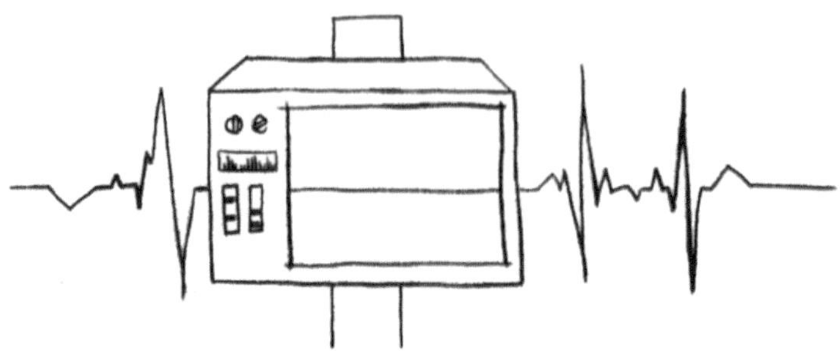

BROKEN HEALER
If your parents are telling you to be a doctor
Don't do it
I repeat *don't do it*
Because you may become a doctor
And heal everyone around you
But yourself
And that is the worst thing you can do
To heal and still be miserable
~Dr. Broken

WELCOME MAT

Home is another word for yelling
Yelling is the word for the laundry you haven't finished
Laundry is another word for lecture
Lecture is another word for incompetent
Incompetent is the silent name you learn to accept
As soon as you realize the boy in your third grade never liked you
The word for hate is your name
Because no one bothers to learn it
Learn is another word for bully
Because the place to grow is the same place to be laughed at
So the journal becomes your therapist
Therapist is another word for delirium
Because getting help is worse
Than suffering in silence
Silence is the word you gave to your love
Who left running with your words
Words become the synonym for tears
Tears is the nickname you give to home.

*~ Inspired by Billy-Ray Belcourt's piece 'Love is a Moontime
    Teaching' which can be found in the Anthology The Next Wave*

PAIRENTS

I'm sorry you only had a year to
Figure if you two were compatible
I'm sorry you had to leave your own house
Because family got too toxic
I'm sorry you had to wait 3 years to start
A family because you had no time to fall in love
I'm sorry you had to leave your country with
A suitcase of clothes on your back
And only the word *Canada* on your lips
But India in your heart
I'm sorry you had to break
Your mother tongue just to say hello
I'm sorry you had to break your heart
In half for some kids
Who are just sorry

~It should be spelled Pairents

IMPORTANT: PLEASE READ

The amount of times
People will downplay your existence
Just so that they can feel significant
Is normal

But don't let anyone get a
                    w
                      a
                        y
                          with it.

STOP RUNNING

If chasing your dream makes you unhappy
Depressed.
Broken.
Tired.
It is no longer a dream.
It is an expectation
That you don't have to *m e e t*

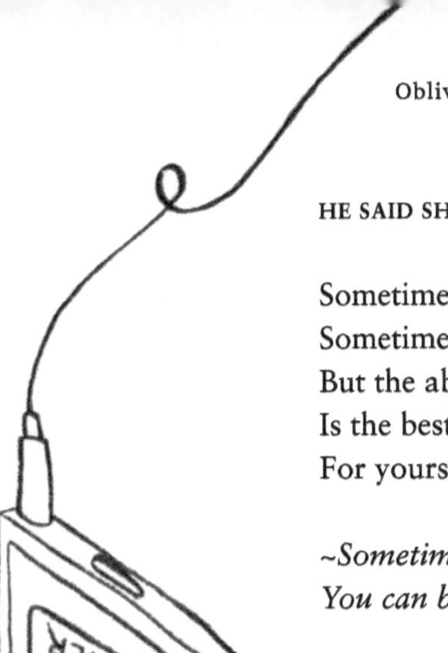

HE SAID SHE SAID

Sometimes it is your fault
Sometimes it's not
But the ability to know when it is—
Is the best thing
For yourself.

~Sometimes people want to be the victim
You can be the victim, or you can be accountable

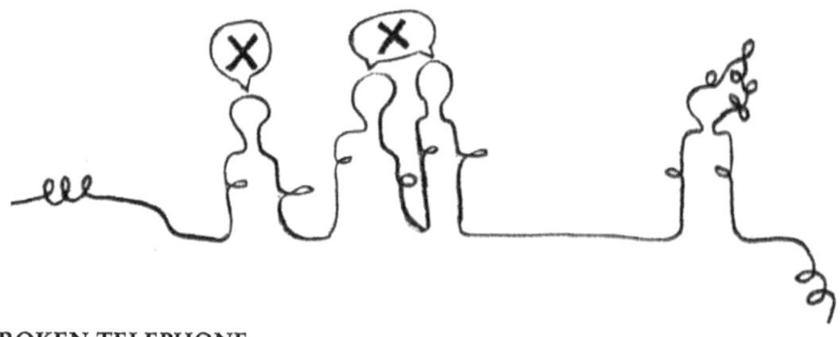

BROKEN TELEPHONE

Sometimes you'll sit to judge
And whisper because it is
What people do
But it is really when people have
Nothing better to do

-Your life has more meaning than living life through other people

PERIOD

My biggest fear is not that I won't be enough
It's that I'll be reduced to a mere
Anecdote
Simply
A myth
Once I leave you
I'll become just
The girl who wrote this
The girl who said this
The girl who did this
The girl who is depressed
The girl who fell for the altar boy
How unfair is it that my present
Will just be a funny story in the past
As if
I'm not the same girl who makes you smile
I'm not the same girl who's fighting her own war
I'm not the same girl who believes other girls aren't my competition
They are my allies
I did not come into this world by
Convenience
Just to be the story you listen to with bitter tea and then forget
Doesn't my name bring light to your eyes
Do I not make your mouth water
Does my history matter so much more than my present
It needs to be whispered into a rumor
As if my sins have become public indecency for society
As if my anxiety shows weakness
As if my mistakes give others a reason to laugh
As if my life holds no significant meaning but to a mere sentence
The girl who...
Couldn't finish this sentence

-2019 Toronto Poetry Slam piece

PHONY

Boys can't stay
Longer than a month
Even if he whispers *"I'll stay the year... I hope"*
They don't understand time
Like we do
For them today is tomorrow
But tomorrow never comes
Until he realizes he is stuck in the
Rabbit hole
And wants to be friends
Instead
You are stuck with 2-word texts left on read
Bed is the only word they comprehend
But only if you are on it
I look back at our texts and think
Was it all pretend
Looks like you blew me off for a job
Yet became one instead

~Letters to my ex

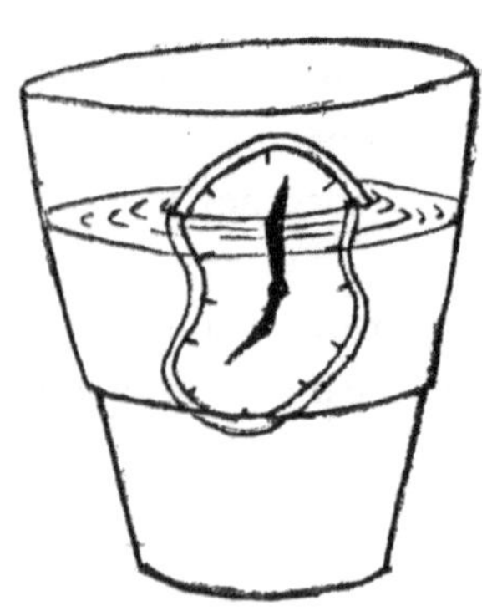

INJUSTICE

It is so unfair
That the people who slice your heart in two
Live on to be immortal in these words
In so many stories
Their betrayal forever lies in so many pages
It breathes around you
Lives on in you
Why should they live on
When they broke you first

MORALS

All my life I've seen religion
Confined to a ritual
A mere five minutes
Or
A big celebration
That has lost its meaning
Where is religion on the street?
On the train
In our friends
In our family
We can close our eyes our whole life
Perform ritual after ritual
But if religion equals ignorance
And it is used to balance ~~our sins~~
And if religion can't find its way into our actions
In our mornings and evenings
In our good deeds
In our forgiveness
Then religion is as useless
As our hope for *change*

THE HARDEST THING

Running around without a Hijab
And calling myself a Muslim

Bare skin exposing my legs and midriff
And calling myself a Muslim

Ignoring my classmate's threats to convert
And calling myself a Muslim

With the fall of the towers and the rise of ISIS
And calling myself a Muslim

Sipping the effect of my first drink
And calling myself a Muslim

Inhaling the first cigarette
And calling myself a Muslim

My body is not Muslim
My actions aren't either
But you don't get
To decide my religion
The hardest thing is
I *do*

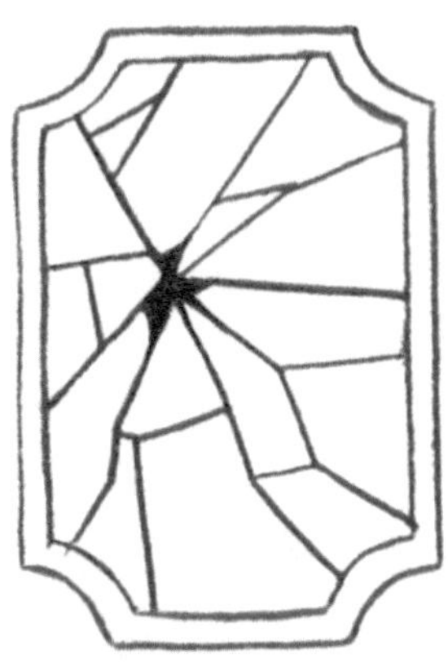

MOMENTUM

You told me you have these *moments*
With other girls
But you won't do anything about it
How can you say *that*
When every moment I think of you
The moon comes out just to remind my eyes
To say your name
So how can you say that
When I showed you every moment of me
And every single eon has led up to loving you
I know some part of you likes it
But I know you love me more
So please tell me
You'll choose me over these *moments*
Because I'd do anything to have a moment
With you

-Quarantine Lover (03.29.2020)

DISTANCING LOVE

I wish instead of turning around and not facing you
I'd stay in your arms to see your face
And give you all the love I can't give you now
I'd find your heartbeat and tell it to
Keep beating for the times
We'd be apart for
I know you're only
11 minutes away
But you know I'd run to you
Even if that means I have to
Leave everything behind
Because when I love
I love enough for two
I know girls haven't treated you
Like the king you are
But I will
Because baby we're both so broken
And that is why we love so hard

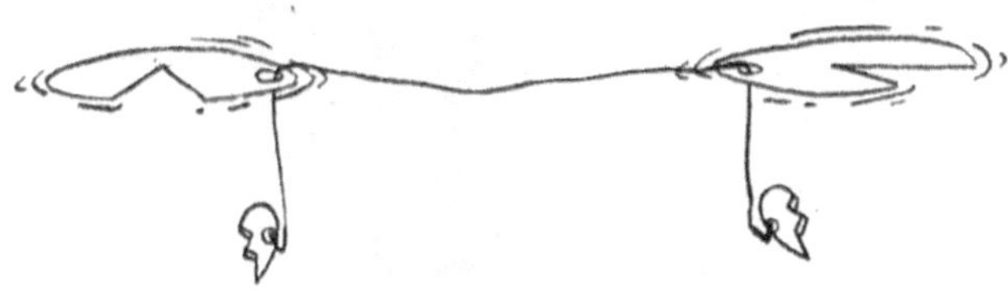

MASTERPIECE

If only life could be a picture
Or a painting
Then we could tell God
Where and what colors
We planned
And God wouldn't laugh
But life is more
Spontaneous
Deep
Transient
It will make you feel so many emotions
On your bathroom floor
In just a
Split
Second
You'll feel like you've seen
The whole world fight
Just in your living room
And one moment
You'll feel on top of the world
While lying on the ground
With mud on your hands and grass at your feet
And that is how life
Paints a
Picture for
You

PUSHOVER!

Every new lockdown I want to push you away
And not speak to you
Because I can't see your face on a screen anymore
I'm tired of this 2-dimensional relationship
How long can I love you from afar
Before it's too far
I love you more than myself
But the world won't let me
So I push you away
Because if I can't have all of you
I'm tired of settling for a remote version of you

OLDEST CHILD.

How do you love if you grew up with it being broken
Silence was the first word I learned
So what does it mean to speak up
When your existence is mere breath?
They were doing the best they could
Unknowingly by making me smaller
And I did become small
So small I ran away
And fixated on school
School broke up with me
Blood came into the picture
It didn't get any better
I remember crying at graduation
Told I was a child but expected to be an adult
I'm called the favourite daughter
But the most scrutinized
And it never is enough
Every year you become better
You make more money
And love them better
But it's never enough
I don't know how to love
If I grew up with it being broken

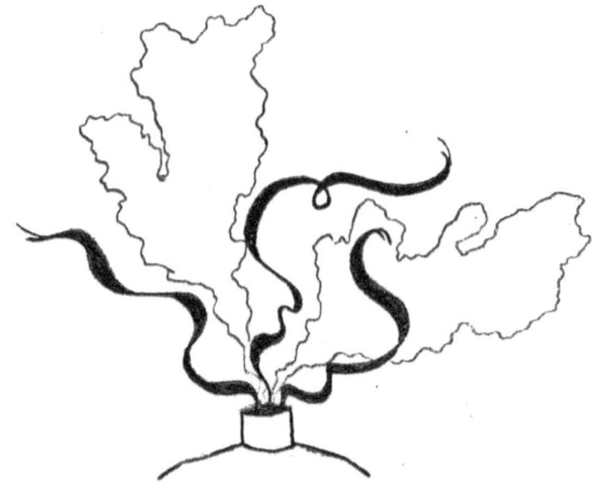

CLOSED SPACE

This space
It has broken lovers
People who
Imagined a future together
But the space keeps changing
Smaller some days and
Some days infinite
And no one knows how long they can love from afar
It's pushing lovers who've come through on the other side
Down the well
And testing them repeatedly
This space isn't going away
It's pushing closer lovers away
And further lovers apart
This space is too close
Too close to space apart

BLOOD*LINE*

What do you do
When the sister you love so dearly
Cuts lines into twos
And you find scars shamed away
And you can't take her pain
But you try
So you lay there awake
Trying to figure out when it became your fault
Because you are her bloodline
And all you see are blood lines
Now you can't tell her life is more than just the masks and two years of
staying at home
But how can you muster up the courage to say you're sorry for the past
you've been
Or for the fights you have
When you should have been on her side
But you didn't
And now lie awake at 1:41 am
Trying to find the words
To apologize for giving her pain
When you should have taken it away

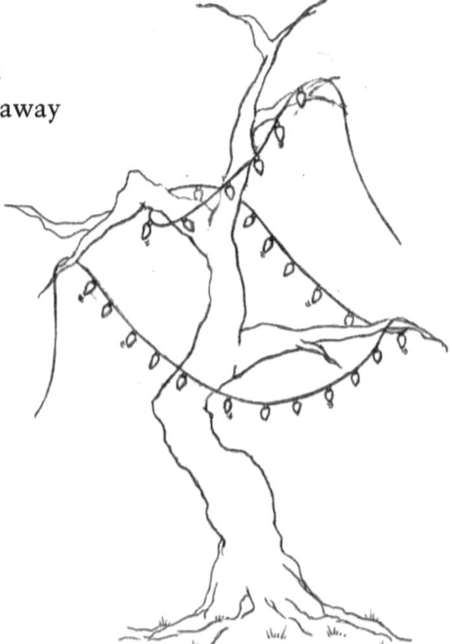

OBLIVIOUS

What if he isn't the one
And he's just waiting for one
And I'm someone to fill his days and nights in his anticipation
Until the right one comes along
How do I know what goes on his head
When I tell him forever is incomplete without him and his silence tells
me he doesn't know
How do I tell him we won't become our parents
I won't repeat history, I promise
How do I tell him this time we'll be different
And our love isn't so delicate
How do I tell him all this when he doesn't believe it
I know I see him in my tomorrows but his calendar isn't that far ahead
How do I know he's not just tolerating this
For something better
What if he's the one but oblivious
Is he the one but doesn't know it yet

UNWANTED
You felt unwanted
Your entire life
Like a doormat that's just too easy
And so, you let people walk over and comment and notice
Your oily hair
That secret birth mark
Your skin color that's just too tan
Your religion that's too problematic
Your talents that are just too much
Your body that's just not skinny
No matter how hard you try
You're told no one wants
You
So, you concoct a reality that no one will love you
convincing yourself it's true
And it's takes 2 years stuck in your home
To realize you were all the stones, pearls and planets, mixed with
the stars and pieces of the universe combined to create this being
for anyone to make you feel that way
And you promise to never look back and remember
But when some song or melody that reminds you were a doormat
And so weak
You cry a little inside
Because you're told you're nothing
When you were actually priceless

UNFINISHED/WAITING

I'm still here waiting for life to resume
Sometime between getting the vaccine
And making plans with friends that aren't on zoom.
I'm still here waiting for everyday to feel different
Not a playlist on repeat
Wanting to make reservations at a new restaurant
Instead of paying uber eats a $2.99 delivery fee
As I look for another promo code
I'm still here right where you left me
Waiting for politicians to place blame on each other for this pandemic
As my hair grows out and I waste time shopping online
Just to feel something
Rationalizing that $900 bi-weekly makes up for my
Life being turned upside down and
Yet I'm still here where COVID-19 left me

You've made it here, I am here with you, in words holding your hands, thank you, thank you, thank you so much, you have no idea what it means for you to hold Oblivion. I know this must have been heavy and difficult, please let yourself feel. Know that I too look back at my poems and smile, cry, laugh and feel just as much as you do. Let me tell you that you are never alone, no matter where you are, you are always enough, and you don't need anyone to tell you otherwise.

Please take the time you need to heal. I will always be forever indebted to you for taking a small piece of my words with you. You are one of the special ones.

This would have never been possible with the people who have supported me from the start. I thank my parents and sister for always being supportive of my dreams, you are my biggest inspiration. This work wouldn't have been possible without my best friend Siham Karamali, you have always been my number one fan, I am so grateful to work with you on Oblivion. I never would have started this chapbook without my boyfriend Yash, you have always believed in me when I was doubtful. I want to express deep gratitude to my friends, Sylvie Stojanovski, Samira Ahmed, Daniel Gomes, Mariam Ansari, Avleen Grewal, and professors Catriona Wright, and Daniel Scott Tysdal. I am forever grateful to everyone supporting me in my writing journey. To every single follower, friend, reader, acquaintance and stranger, you are the reason I write.

Thank you to The Soapbox Press for making my dream come true.

Please feel free to connect with me on my socials! I'd love to hear from you.

Instagram: @lamiafirasta/@lamiart__
YouTube: @lamiart__
Twitter: @LFirasta
TikTok: @lamiart__

For more information about Plume visit us online at:
www.plumepress.com